W9-CFT-414

POWER READING

Reading and Thinking Strategies for Adults
Book 1

DOROTHY RUBIN

CAMBRIDGE Adult Education
Globe Fearon Educational Publisher
Upper Saddle River, New Jersey

Library of Congress Cataloging-in-Publication Data
Rubin, Dorothy.
    Power reading : reading and thinking strategies for adults /
Dorothy Rubin.
      p.   cm.
   ISBN 0-13-184847-X (bk. 1)
   1. Reading (Adult education) 2. Reading—Comprehension
I. Title.
LC5225.R4R83   1995
428.4'071'5—dc20   94-38282
                                            CIP

Executive Editor: Mark Moscowitz
Project Editor: Karen Bernhaut
Production Editor: Rose Kernan
Designer: Fred Dahl
Cover Designer: Marianne Frasco
Project Production Manager: Edward O'Dougherty

©1995 by CAMBRIDGE Adult Education
A Division of Simon & Schuster
Upper Saddle River, New Jersey 07458

All rights reserved. No part of this book
may be reproduced in any form or by any means
without permission in writing from the publisher.

Printed in the United States of America
10 9 8 7 6 5 4 3 2 1

ISBN 0-13-184847-X

CAMBRIDGE Adult Education
A Division of Simon & Schuster
Upper Saddle River, New Jersey 07458

Contents

UNIT TWO

UNIT THREE

To the Instructor

Power Reading: Reading and Thinking Strategies for Adults is a three-book series dedicated to helping adults at the pre-GED level develop the reading comprehension skills and strategies they need to deal with practical problems in their daily lives and in the workplace. It will help adult learners achieve the literacy goals set forth for the 21st century.

To carry out this aim, each of the three books presents continuing realistic adult situations along with the reading skills. The situations are interesting stories with recurring characters in the roles of spouses, parents, consumers, tenants, and employees. The life themes of the stories are those to which adults can readily relate. The stories and passages that are used to help students gain the presented skills and strategies are informative, dramatic, and enjoyable.

There are three units in each book containing lessons that highlight a specific reading comprehension skill with strategies to achieve that skill. There are various examples and explanations to help adult learners gain insight into the material presented. Each lesson also contains practices to help adult learners gain proficiency in the presented skill and strategy.

Book 1 focuses on finding the main idea of a paragraph, a very important skill which is difficult for many students. For this reason, instruction in Book 1 leads up to the main idea through simpler comprehension skills; finding details that answer "the five Ws" (Who? What? When? Where? Why?), finding details that answer specific questions, restating one or two sentences, restating three or more sentences, and finding the topic of a paragraph.

Finding and expressing the main idea is a highly useful skill for adult learners in both reading and writing. As a result, reading and writing are combined in the instruction of Book 1, as well as in the other books of the series. In reading, the ability to locate or state the main idea helps students to understand what they have read and to remember it. In writing, an understanding of the main idea enables students to organize their thoughts into clear and logical paragraphs.

In Book 1, therefore, adult learners are taken step by step through all those skills and strategies they need to be able to figure out the main idea of a paragraph. Throughout the series, instruction is presented in a carefully paced, incremental way—a user-friendly design for the pre-GED student.

Power Reading is based on sound learning principles and is devised to keep the adult learner actively engaged throughout. It encourages self-pacing and immediate feedback and provides graduated levels of difficulty, distributed practice, and selections based on adult interests. It also teaches generalizations where applicable.

The structure of *Power Reading* makes it versatile. It can be used in conventional classroom settings, in tutorial situations and clinics, or by students working semi-independently.

UNIT ONE

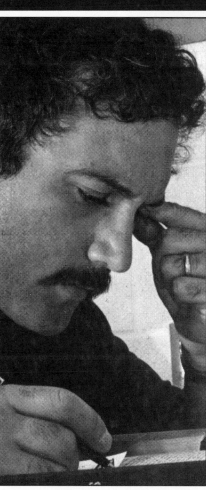

LESSON 1

ANSWERING THE BASIC QUESTIONS ABOUT SOMETHING YOU READ: WHO? WHAT? WHEN? WHERE? WHY?

We usually read for two reasons—for pleasure or to find information about something. Often, we read for both reasons. When you read, it is important to be able to find specific pieces of information, called facts or **details** and to be able to remember them. Many tests you will take—for jobs, for driver's licenses, for courses in schools and training programs—will ask you to state details about what you have read. When you read for pleasure, you will often talk about it with friends, sharing your enjoyment of details and discussing their meaning. The more you can remember, the more you will enjoy what you read and the better able you will be to talk about it and make use of it.

Most details in your reading answer five basic questions:

Who?

What?

When?

Where?

Why?

Read the following paragraph and answer the questions about it.

~~Germaine~~ Sally is a hardworking person. She gets up at 6:00 A.M. because she has a lot to do before she goes to work. Every morning she has to straighten up and prepare breakfast for her two children. She drives her children to day care and then goes to work at 8:30 A.M. After work, she picks up her children, goes food shopping, and then goes home to prepare dinner, clean up, do the wash, and so on. ~~Germaine~~ also goes to school two nights a week. Sally

1. Who is doing the activities?

GO ON TO THE NEXT PAGE.

2. What does she do two nights a week?

3. When does she get up in the morning?

4. Where does she take her children before she goes to work?

5. Why does she get up so early when work starts at 8:30?

This paragraph contains different kinds of details. The answer to the first question is the name of a person: Germaine. The answer to the second question tells you an activity, what she does two nights a week—she goes to school. The answer to the third question is a number—the specific time she gets up in the morning, 6:00 A.M. The answer to the fourth question identifies a place, the place where Germaine takes her children before she goes to work—day care. The answer to the last question tells you why Germaine gets up so early—she has a lot to do before she goes to work.

You already take in these different kinds of information in your daily reading of newspapers, magazines, and books. All you need to do is practice this skill of noticing details and remembering them so that you can put it to practical use in your study and your work.

In the following Practices, you can develop this skill further.

GO ON TO THE NEXT PAGE.

Practice 1

> "I'm a lucky man," thought Mario. "Molly is a good wife and we have two nice children. My biggest piece of luck is that last week I got a good job that pays well. My boss likes me, and I like my work. Soon, we will be able to move to a larger apartment outside the city because we are saving something out of every paycheck."

1. Who is the speaker in the paragraph?

2. Wh_____of luck"?

3. Wh_____of luck"?

4. Wh

5. Why will he be able to move to a larger apartment?

LIFE SKILLS DISCUSSION QUESTIONS

1. Where could Mario go to look for a job if he needed to?

2. How might Mario find a larger apartment?

STOP   *CHECK ANSWERS ON PAGE 115.*

Practice 2

Mario was very upset. He had been laid off from his job. He couldn't believe he was being let go. Just last week his boss had said, "Mario, you are a good worker. I am happy with your work."

After hearing that, Mario thought he might be getting a raise. Instead, on Monday the boss had asked him into his office and told him that he was laid off. He was in shock. "How could this have happened?" he asked a co-worker. "What will I say to my wife?"

1. Who told Mario that he was happy with his work?

2. What has happened to Mario?

3. When did this event happen?

4. Where was Mario told about his job situation?

5. Why was Mario in shock about what his boss told him?

LIFE SKILLS DISCUSSION QUESTIONS

1. What are fair reasons for being fired? What are unfair reasons?

2. What are fair reasons for being promoted? What are unfair reasons?

STOP *CHECK ANSWERS ON PAGE 115.*

Practice 3

> Mario decided to speak to his boss at the end of the day on Monday. He wanted to know why he had been laid off. He went to his boss's office. "Mr. Cortez," Mario said, "just last week you told me that I was a good worker. You said you were happy with me."
>
> "I am," said Mr. Cortez. "I am not unhappy with you or your work. I have no choice. Business is not good. I am sad to lose such a good worker as you. However, I have to let go the last person I hired. Unfortunately, you are that person."

1. To whom did Mario talk about losing his job? (Give the person's name.)

2. Why did Mario want to talk to this person about losing his job?

3. What reason was Mario given for being let go?

4. When did Mario go to talk about losing his job?

5. Where did Mario talk about losing his job?

GO ON TO THE NEXT PAGE.

1. Do you think it is fair to fire the last person hired? Explain.

2. What do you think Mario might ask his boss to do to help him find another job?

STOP *CHECK ANSWERS ON PAGE 115.*

Practice 4

> Mario left Mr. Cortez's office in a very depressed mood. He still couldn't believe that he had lost his job. He felt as if his whole world had fallen apart. He felt ill. His mouth was dry and his hands were sweaty. Even though it was warm, he felt cold at times, and his heart beat faster than usual.
>
> Sam, one of his co-workers, saw him in the coffee shop and said, "What's the matter? Are you all right? You look terrible."
>
> Mario looked at him sadly and gave him a weak smile. "No, Sam," he said, "I just need to get some fresh air."

1. Whom did Mario meet after he left the boss's office?

2. What did the person he met say to Mario?

3. Where did the person he met see Mario?

4. What was Mario's mood when he met this person?

5. Why was Mario in such a terrible state of mind?

GO ON TO THE NEXT PAGE.

1. What professional person could Mario go to for help and advice?

2. What are some signs or symptoms of stress (other than those mentioned in the passage)?

STOP *CHECK ANSWERS ON PAGE 115.*

Practice 5

> Mario decided to walk home rather than take a bus. He wanted some time to think. He wanted to figure out how and when to tell the news to his wife, Molly. Should he wait until after they had eaten dinner? Should he wait until after the children were in bed? Should he come out and say, "Hi, dear, I just lost my job!" Should he pretend that everything was fine and not tell her at all? He felt confused.

1. Whom did Mario think of telling about what had happened?

2. What did Mario decide to do right after work?

3. When did he think he should tell the person? (There are three possible answers; give one.)

4. Where did Mario go when he left the coffee shop?

5. Why did Mario walk rather than take the bus? (There is more than one correct answer; give one.)

GO ON TO THE NEXT PAGE.

11

1. If Mario tells Molly what has happened, what do you think Molly will say?

2. What do you think would be the best response—that is, what do you think would help Mario the most?

3. If Mario does not tell Molly what has happened, what do you think might happen?

STOP *CHECK ANSWERS ON PAGE 115.*

LESSON 2
READING TO FIND DETAILS

In Lesson 1, you practiced remembering details that you noticed as you read along in order to answer questions later. You did not have questions about the paragraph before you started reading it because you had no idea what it was going to be about.

In your daily reading, however, you often have an idea of the content you are about to read because you are reading it to find a specific piece of information. For instance, we read the weather report to find out what the temperatures will be today or whether it will rain. We look at the movie or television sections to see what shows are on at certain times. We read advertisements to see what new products are available and what their prices are.

Even when we are not looking for information but reading for pleasure, we read to find out what the headline or the title of a piece of writing means. For instance, look at the following paragraph. Seeing this headline, you probably would read to find out what a single mother's goals are.

WHAT ARE A SINGLE MOTHER'S GOALS IN LIFE?

Kyung is a single mother with two children. She wants to give them a good start in life so that they can have more than she has. She knows the importance of a good education. However, Kyung did not finish high school because she didn't like it. She will make sure that her children study hard and finish school.

When you read the title of this paragraph, "A Single Mother's Goals in Life," you ask yourself the "What" question from the Five Ws approach you used in Lesson 1: What are the single mother's goals in life?

Goals are things a person wants to achieve. What does Kyung want to achieve? In the second sentence, we are told that she wants her children to have a "good start in life so that they can have more than she has had": that is one goal. In the third sentence, we are told that "she knows the importance of a good education" and, in the last sentence, that "she will make sure that her children study

GO ON TO THE NEXT PAGE.

hard and finish school." So her other goal is for her children to get a high school education.

Remembering Details Accurately

If you are a good reader, you will be able to tell if someone says something untrue about the article, even if you do not remember all the details. For example, if someone said that Kyung wanted her children to quit school and go to work, you would know immediately the statement was false. On the other hand, if someone said that Kyung did not like high school, you would know that this was a true statement.

See if you can answer the following True or False statements. Put a T by true statements and an F by false ones.

1. Kyung liked school. _____

2. Kyung has two children. _____

3. Kyung finished high school. _____

4. Kyung has remarried. _____

LIFE SKILLS DISCUSSION QUESTION

What can Kyung do to help her children stay in school?

Read the following Practice selections and try to find the detail that will answer the question its title raises in your mind. Then answer the True/False questions that test how many details you can remember accurately.

STOP *CHECK ANSWERS ON PAGE 115.*

> Mario's wife, Molly, was very upset when she heard that he had lost his job. However, she knew it was not his fault, so she was very sympathetic and helpful. She told him, "You must do something every day to find a new job."
>
> "Like what?" asked Mario.
>
> "Well," said Molly, "you can look in the want ads in the newspapers. You can also start networking."
>
> "What do you mean by networking?" asked Mario.
>
> "Networking means that you call everyone you know to find out if they can give you help in finding a new job," Molly explained.
>
> "Sounds great," said Mario. "I'll start right away."

Networking is

Read the following statements. Put a T by the true statements and an F by the false statements.

1. Mario is willing to listen to advice. _____

2. Molly says that she will get a job to replace Mario's job. _____

3. Molly tells Mario to look at the want ads. _____

4. Molly says that Mario's friends will give him a job. _____

5. Molly says Mario must do something every day to look for a new job. _____

LIFE SKILLS DISCUSSION QUESTION

Discuss different ways to network (for example, to find a job, to make a major purchase, to expand your social life, to choose a school, to plan a vacation, and so on).

STOP   *CHECK ANSWERS ON PAGE 115.*

That same night, Mario sat down and began phoning his friends. He told them that he had lost his job and that he needed their help. He asked them if they knew of any jobs that were available where they worked. He also asked them if they knew of anyone who would help him. He told them to please keep their eyes and ears open and to let him know if they heard of any open position. Mario was on the phone for hours. He didn't realize how many friends he had.

When he networked, Mario

Read the following statements. Put a T by the true statements and an F by the false statements.

1. Mario was trying hard to find a job. _____

2. Molly gave Mario the names of people to call. _____

3. Mario realized that he did not have many friends. _____

4. Mario spent a lot of time on the phone looking for work. _____

5. Mario asked Molly to make phone calls, too. _____

LIFE SKILLS DISCUSSION QUESTION

What are some things Mario can do to help make his networking on the phone easier?

STOP   *CHECK ANSWERS ON PAGE 115.*

WHAT JOB OPENING DID MARIO FIND BY NETWORKING?

Mario was very excited. He couldn't believe his good luck. His networking had paid off. A friend of his called him back and told him that she had heard that the Clark Company was hiring 10 new trainees. She also said that the company was looking for someone with Mario's job experience. Mario called the Clark Company to find out about the position. The person there told him to come down and fill out a job application. Mario went and filled one out right away. The next week, Mr. Duvall, the Area Supervisor for the Clark Company, phoned Mario to set up an interview.

By networking, Mario found

Read the following statements. Put a T by the true statements and an F by the false statements.

1. Mario's friend paid someone to tell her about the job opening. _____

2. Mario's job experience does not relate to the new job. _____

3. Mario filled out a job application. _____

4. A supervisor at the company phoned Mario. _____

5. Mr. Duvall set up an interview with Mario. _____

LIFE SKILLS DISCUSSION QUESTION

Discuss how Mario should dress for his interview.

STOP *CHECK ANSWERS ON PAGE 115.*

HOW DID MARIO FEEL ABOUT THE UPCOMING INTERVIEW?

The night before the interview Mario could hardly sleep. When the alarm went off, he already was awake. Since he was too excited to eat, he just had a cup of coffee. Mario dressed carefully. He picked out a white shirt and a nice suit to wear. Mario made sure that his shoes were polished and that he looked good. He looked at the clock. His interview was at 9:00 that morning. It would only take him 15 minutes to get there by bus, and it was only 8:00 A.M., but he decided to leave, anyway.

Before the interview, Mario felt

Read the following statements. Put a T by the true statements and an F by the false ones.

1. Mario slept well the night before the interview. _____

2. Mario dressed carefully for the interview. _____

3. Molly picked out what Mario would wear for the interview. _____

4. Mario was too nervous to eat anything before his interview. _____

5. Mario did not leave enough time to get to his interview. _____

GO ON TO THE NEXT PAGE.

LIFE SKILLS DISCUSSION QUESTIONS

    1. Did Mario do everything needed to get ready for his interview? Explain.

    2. How would you get ready for an interview?

STOP   *CHECK ANSWERS ON PAGE 115.*

WHAT MISTAKE DID MARIO MAKE IN HIS INTERVIEW?

At his interview, Mr. Duvall smiled, shook hands with him, and asked him to sit down. He began asking Mario questions about his job experience. He said that Mario answered these questions very well.

"So," he said, "why do you want to come to work for us?"

"Well," Mario answered, "I, well, this would be a good company to work for."

"Why?" asked Mr. Duvall.

"I'm not sure," replied Mario.

Mr. Duvall stood up and said, "Thanks for coming in."

As Mario left, he said to himself: "One thing I know. In the next interview, I will be better prepared."

In his interview, Mario's mistake was

Read the following statements. Put a T by the true statements and an F by the false ones.

1. Mr. Duvall did not like any of Mario's answers. _____

2. Mario was sure of himself at the interview. _____

3. Mr. Duvall was polite during the interview. _____

4. Mario did not want to go to any more interviews. _____

5. Mario learned something from the interview. _____

LIFE SKILLS DISCUSSION QUESTION

How do you think you should behave during an interview? Explain.

STOP *CHECK ANSWERS ON PAGE 115.*

LESSON 3
RESTATING ONE OR TWO SENTENCES

Every day you have to tell people about something in your own words. At work, someone may ask you about part of your job. You may read an article or a movie review and a friend may ask, "What did it say?"

Look at this example:

Most of the excitement in the movie comes from the intense love relationship between the male and female leads.

You could state this again in these words:

The love story is the best thing about the movie.

One way to test whether you have understood something you have read is to see if you can state the meaning of it clearly in your own words.

For instance, look at this statement:

That night, Mario began phoning his friends to tell them that he had lost his job and to ask them if they knew of any jobs that were available.

Now look at this restatement of this statement:

Mario asked his friends to help him find a new job.

Restatements are often simpler than the original statement—like the one above. However, they need to be complete. What is wrong with the above restatement? It is incomplete: it leaves out the fact that Mario has lost his job. Look at this revision of it:

Mario told his friends that he had lost his job and asked them to help him find a new one.

Restatements also need to be correct and clear. Look at this statement:

Through networking, a friend of his called Mario back and told him that the Clark Company was hiring ten new trainees.

Now look at this restatement of it:

A friend of Mario's told him about a job.

GO ON TO THE NEXT PAGE.

What is wrong with this restatement? It is incomplete and inaccurate. It is not complete because it does not mention networking. It is also inaccurate, because it says that Mario found out about one job, when in fact he found out about ten possible jobs.

Here is a better restatement:

Through networking, Mario learned about ten possible jobs.

Read the following Practice passages and answer the restatement questions about them.

GO ON TO THE NEXT PAGE.

When Mario got home, his wife Molly was anxiously waiting to hear what had happened. "How did it go?" she asked.

"Well," said Mario, "I know I won't get the job."

"What do you mean you won't get the job?" asked Molly. "You just went for the interview. They take time deciding whom they will hire."

"Trust me, Molly," said Mario, "they won't hire me."

Molly told him to tell her everything that had happened at the interview. He told her that he knew he looked good and answered most of the questions well. However he did not know enough about the company. Molly said that he should not feel so bad because she was sure he would get a job somewhere else.

1. Which of the following is the best restatement of Molly's statement: "They take time deciding whom they will hire."

   a. Molly thinks it is too early to tell if Mario got the job.

   b. Molly thinks Mario took too much time at the interview.

   c. Molly wants Mario to try to get a different job.

2. Which of the following is the best restatement of the last sentence?

   a. Molly doesn't think Mario did anything wrong at the interview.

   b. Molly thinks Mario misunderstood the interviewer.

   c. Molly doesn't think the interview is a fair test of Mario's ability.

GO ON TO THE NEXT PAGE.

3. Read the following statements. Put a T by the statements that are true and an F by those that are false.

   a. Mario was certain he was not going to get the job at the Clark Company. _____

   b. Mario refused to tell Molly anything about the interview. _____

   c. Molly worried about the outcome of Mario's interview. _____

   d. Mario wanted another interview at the Clark Company. _____

   e. Molly told Mario he could find another job. _____

LIFE SKILLS DISCUSSION QUESTION

Why is it important to have a support system (for example, a partner to support you while you look for a job)?

STOP *CHECK ANSWERS ON PAGE 116.*

Mario wasn't surprised that he did not get the job at the Clark Company because he knew he wasn't prepared for the interview. "I was so excited about getting the interview that I didn't try to find out anything about the company," he said to himself.

Mario's failure taught him some important things about interviewing. He had to find out as much as he could about the company hiring people. He had to make sure that he knew what the company did and how large it was. He had to think about what questions the interviewer might ask and practice answering them.

1. Which of the following is the best restatement of the first sentence of the passage?

    a. Mario never expected to get the job he interviewed for.

    b. Mario wasn't really interested in the job he interviewed for.

    c. Mario did not get the job because he didn't get ready for the interview.

2. Which of the following is the best restatement of the last sentence of the passage?

    a. Mario should find out who the interviewer is before an interview.

    b. Mario should find out the interview questions before an interview.

    c. Mario should practice being interviewed before an interview.

GO ON TO THE NEXT PAGE.

3. Read the following statements. Put a T by the statements that are true and an F by those that are false.

a. Mario blamed the interviewer for not getting the job. _____

b. Mario was not well prepared for the interview. _____

c. Mario learned that the way he dressed for the interview was wrong. _____

d. Mario was shocked when he did not get the job. _____

e. Mario will use what he has learned to go for another interview at the Clark Company. _____

LIFE SKILLS DISCUSSION QUESTION

How could Mario get information about the company that is interviewing him for a job?

STOP *CHECK ANSWERS ON PAGE 116.*

HOW MARIO GETS MONEY WHILE OUT OF WORK

"You know, Mario," Molly said several weeks later, "we're lucky that you're collecting some money while you're out of work."

"I know," replied Mario, "I was thinking the same thing just the other day. It's a good thing I'm collecting unemployment compensation while I'm looking for a job. At least we have some money coming in every week. That way we don't have to use up all our savings. The people at my old job told me to apply for unemployment insurance compensation right away when I lost my job. They said I would be able to get it because I had worked for more than twenty weeks during the year. Also, my old employer paid into a fund for unemployment insurance."

"He doesn't give you a lot," Molly said. "He's stingy."

"No," Mario said, "that isn't the reason. He did not have to put in so much because I did not have a very good salary. The amount you get in compensation depends on how much you made while you were working."

1. Which of the following is the best restatement of the last sentence?

   a. You get part of your compensation while you are still working.

   b. How much compensation you get depends on how long you have worked.

   c. Your level of compensation depends on your pay while working.

GO ON TO THE NEXT PAGE.

2. Read the following statements. Put a T by the statements that are true and an F by those that are false.

    a. Molly thought that Mario's old employer must be stingy. _____

    b. Mario had worked more than twenty weeks during the year. _____

    c. At first, Mario got too much unemployment insurance money. _____

    d. Mario applied for unemployment insurance right after he lost his job. _____

    e. Part of Mario's unemployment insurance money came from his savings. _____

LIFE SKILLS DISCUSSION QUESTION

How might unemployment compensation be important for someone (that is, how could it help you while out of work)? Explain.

STOP   *CHECK ANSWERS ON PAGE 116.*

HOW DOES MARIO FEEL ABOUT BEING UNEMPLOYED?

Mario has been out of work for six months. He is beginning to feel sorry for himself because he can't find another job. Everywhere he goes, he hears the same story. Employers are laying off workers because they need to make more profits. They are not rehiring. One Monday morning, when Molly called him to come to breakfast, Mario did not feel like getting out of bed. He pulled the covers over his head and ignored her. "What's the use," he thought to himself. "I'll probably never get a job again. Soon we'll use up all our money. I won't get any more unemployment compensation. We'll become just another homeless family."

1. Which of the following is the best restatement of Mario's statements: "What's the use   I'll probably never get a job again."

   a. Mario thinks employers are prejudiced against him. ____

   b. Mario feels that he is a helpless victim. ____

   c. Mario does not feel that Molly is helping him enough. ____

2. Read the following statements. Put a T by the statements that are true and an F by those that are false.

   a. Mario is beginning to feel defeated. _____

   b. Mario has been out of work for 16 weeks. _____

   c. Mario won't get out of bed because he's lazy. _____

LIFE SKILLS DISCUSSION QUESTION

How do you think you would feel—and behave—in Mario's place?

STOP   *CHECK ANSWERS ON PAGE 116.*

HOW DOES MOLLY REACT TO MARIO'S BEHAVIOR?

> That Monday morning, when Mario did not get out of bed, Molly came into the bedroom. She looked at him and said, "Mario, get out of bed. I know what you're thinking, but it's not true. You will find another job. I know that you've been trying very hard. You've called places that hire workers and looked at lots of want ads. So far, it hasn't helped. But six months is not such a long time to be out of work. That's why you can get unemployment compensation for at least twenty-six weeks. Please, get out of bed. The children will be frightened if you stay in bed so late. They will think you are sick. Let's look at the Help Wanted ads together."

1. What is the best restatement of Molly's statements: "I know what you're thinking, but it's not true. You will find another job."

   a. Molly wants Mario to believe he will have success.

   b. Molly thinks Mario is mentally sick.

   c. Molly thinks Mario is only pretending to be depressed.

2. Which of the following is the best restatement of Molly's statements; "The children will be frightened if you stay in bed so late. They will think you are sick."

   a. Molly thinks Mario's illness may be passed on to their children if he does not make an effort to get well.

   b. Molly is afraid Mario's illness will get worse if he does not get out of bed.

   c. Molly thinks the children will be afraid and believe Mario is ill if he stays in bed.

GO ON TO THE NEXT PAGE.

3. Read the following statements. Put a T by the statements that are true and an F by those that are false.

a. Molly won't let Mario feel sorry for himself. _____

b. Mario won't get out of bed because he is tired. _____

c. Molly does not think Mario has been unemployed very long. _____

d. Molly offers to help Mario find a job. _____

e. Mario's children have become frightened of him. _____

LIFE SKILLS DISCUSSION QUESTION

What are other ways besides networking and newspaper ads that Mario can use to look for a job?

STOP *CHECK ANSWERS ON PAGE 116.*

UNIT TWO

LESSON 4

RESTATING THREE OR MORE SENTENCES

In the last lesson, you learned about restating information. You saw that sometimes the restatement just puts a sentence into different words. Other restatements put the information and meaning of a couple of sentences into a new statement.

In this lesson, we will be restating a larger group of sentences into a single restatement.

Look at this example:

Rental car companies now refuse to rent cars to people with poor driving records. They will not rent to people who have had an accident in the last three years. They also will not rent cars to anyone who has been found guilty of driving while drunk or using drugs.

A short restatement of these sentences might be the following:

Rental car companies will not rent cars to people who have had recent accidents or who drive while drunk or on drugs.

An even simpler restatement might be:

Rental car companies will not rent cars to people they think are bad drivers.

Here is what we did to get this shorter restatement: "Bad drivers" is a way of putting together the information and meaning of "people with poor driving records" (sentence 1), "people who have had an accident in the last three years" (sentence 2), and "anyone found guilty of driving while drunk or using drugs" (sentence 3).

It is harder to write a restatement of three or more sentences than it is to restate only one or two sentences because this larger restatement includes more information. Still, you are doing the same thing as when you are restating one sentence. See if you can write a restatement of the following:

Many people use their credit cards too much. People used to charge only large purchases, such as major home appliances, major pieces of

GO ON TO THE NEXT PAGE.

furniture, or expensive clothes. Now credit cards are used to buy many other items, which might better be paid for in cash, such as dinners, compact discs, audiotapes and videos, books, tickets for concerts, and even movie tickets. As a result, many people live in constant debt and lose a lot of money by paying interest on the debt.

Which of the following is the best brief restatement of the paragraph?

People have started using credit cards to pay interest on money.
Credit cards are now used in unnecessary and wasteful ways.
Credit cards are now used for every part of people's lives.

The paragraph contrasts the old ways of using credit cards with the new ways that are used today—"to buy many other items, which might better be paid for in cash." The result of the new ways, the paragraph says, is "constant debt" and a loss of money through interest payments on the debt.

The second restatement covers this information and meaning best: "unnecessary" refers to "items, which might better be paid for in cash," and "wasteful" refers to the loss of a lot of money in interest payments on debt.

The first and last restatements are inaccurate. The paragraph does not say that credit cards are used to pay interest on debt or that they are used for "every part of people's lives"—such as daily food and transportation, doctor's bills, electricity, laundry, and so on.

Read the following Practice passages and answer the questions about them, using your skill of restating.

GO ON TO THE NEXT PAGE.

When Mario had been out of work for six months, Molly said she wanted to try to get a job. Unemployment compensation was barely enough to feed their family. Her decision upset Mario. "Molly," he said, "we discussed this a lot. We both said we wanted you to stay home until little Eric was in school."

"That is true, but you can stay at home with Eric," said Molly.

"How can I stay home when I am hunting for a job all the time?" asked Mario.

"Maybe we should put Eric in day care," said Molly. "Then I can work and you can look for a job."

"What makes you think you can find a job?" asked Mario.

"I was a waitress before," said Molly. "Restaurants always need waitresses," she said.

1. Which of the following best restates Molly's reasons for wanting to get a job?

   a. They need the money, and she is sure she can get a job.

   b. With a job as a waitress, Molly can earn more than Mario.

   c. They both can work and take turns staying home with Eric.

2. Which of the following best restates Mario's argument against Molly's suggestion?

   a. Mario cannot look for a job and take care of Eric at the same time.

   b. Molly cannot earn enough to pay for day care for Eric.

   c. Molly cannot find a job while Mario looks for work.

GO ON TO THE NEXT PAGE.

3. Read the following statements and put a T by the statements that are true and an F by those that are false.

a. Mario is sure Molly will find a job as a waitress. _____

b. Unemployment compensation does not give much support to their family. _____

c. Molly feels there are always waitress jobs. _____

d. Mario has been out of work for six months. _____

e. Molly's idea about getting a job upsets Mario. _____

LIFE SKILLS DISCUSSION QUESTIONS

1. What would you do about getting a job if you were Molly?

2. What are some ways that you can save money?

STOP   *CHECK ANSWERS ON PAGE 116.*

> Molly has decided not to get a job for now but to save money instead. The best way to save money is to shop carefully. She checks prices to make sure she is getting the best buy. She clips coupons from the newspapers. When she goes to the supermarket, she always takes an envelope full of coupons. In this way, she saves a lot of money. Many coupons are for items she can use to make inexpensive meals, such as noodle or pasta dishes or meatloaves. She also watches for ads in the papers about sales at different supermarkets. She compares the prices and buys the cheapest items at each store. Sometimes she goes to four or five nearby stores so that she can save money.

1. Which of these statements best restates how Molly saves money shopping?

   a. Molly saves money by using coupons and buying large amounts.

   b. Molly saves money by comparing prices and using coupons to make inexpensive meals.

   c. Molly saves money by going to many supermarkets and buying only a few items.

2. Which of the following is the best restatement of the last three sentences of the paragraph?

   a. Molly shops at different supermarkets to find the cheapest prices.

   b. Molly uses newspaper ads to find out about sales at different stores.

   c. With the use of ads to compare prices, Molly finds out about sales at different stores and shops at these.

GO ON TO THE NEXT PAGE.

1. What do you think of Molly's ways of saving money in her shopping?

2. What ways do you use to save money in your shopping?

3. Do you look at the unit price of a product and compare it with the unit price of a similar product of another brand? Why do you think it is important to do this? Explain.

STOP *CHECK ANSWERS ON PAGE 116.*

When Molly shops for groceries, she buys food that is good for her family's health and that does not cost much. She never buys expensive fish or cuts of meat, such as halibut, salmon, lamp chops, or sirloin steaks. Some of the meat she buys can be mixed with other, cheaper food, such as noodles, or other pasta like macaroni. Other meat she buys can be cooked with rice, potatoes, tomatoes, and carrots. In this way, she can get the best value with her grocery money. She also buys a lot of fresh green vegetables. When she buys food in boxes or cans, she always reads the labels. The labels tell her what vitamins each food contains. She does not buy "fast foods" or "junk foods" that are full of fat or sweet foods that are full of sugar. She knows they give quick energy but are not healthy for you.

1. Which of the following best restates the kinds of fish and meat that Molly buys?

   a. Molly only buys inexpensive meat and fish that she can mix with other inexpensive foods.

   b. Molly buys only fish and meat that comes in cans or boxes and can be cooked with fresh green vegetables.

   c. Molly buys only fish and meat that is inexpensive and contains vitamins.

2. Which of the following is the best restatement of the last four sentences of the paragraph?

   a. Molly reads labels carefully and buys only healthful foods.

   b. Molly buys vitamins rather than fatty or sweet foods that are not healthy for you.

   c. Molly buys foods for their vitamins and avoids unhealthful foods.

GO ON TO THE NEXT PAGE.

1. What do you think of Molly's shopping habits?

2. How healthful are the foods you eat? How do you decide what to eat?

STOP *CHECK ANSWERS ON PAGE 116.*

Mario was depressed about his job hunt, so he got some advice from his friend, Pete.

"It seems hopeless," he told Pete. "Employers aren't interested in me. I must not have the skills they need."

"There must be some reason you are not having any luck at all," said Pete. "How do you sound on the phone?" he asked Mario.

"I sound great," said Mario, "I think."

Pete began to ask Mario a series of questions: "Do you sound sure of yourself or do you sound a little bit scared? Do you phone from a quiet place? Do you have a pencil and paper ready in case they give you information? Do you have a list of all your past jobs in front of you? Do you show that you are really interested and know something about the company?"

Mario looked sad. "I guess not," he answered. "I don't like to push myself."

"You have to push yourself," said Pete. "You have to present yourself as someone who is ready to start work."

1. Which of the following is the best restatement of Mario's feelings about his job hunt? ("It seems hopeless. Employers aren't interested in me. I must not have the skills they need.")

   a. Mario believes employers must think he is basically stupid.

   b. Mario feels he is too depressed to make a good impression on employers.

   c. Mario thinks employers must want something he does not have to offer.

GO ON TO THE NEXT PAGE.

2. Which of the following best restates this dialogue at the end of the selection: "I don't like to push myself," said Mario "You have to push yourself," said Pete. "You have to present yourself as someone who is ready to start work."

   a. Pete wants Mario to get ready for work more often.

   b. Pete believes Mario is not interested in finding work.

   c. Pete wants Mario to show how much he wants to work.

3. How would you restate the advice that Pete gives to Mario about how he should behave when phoning employers?

LIFE SKILLS DISCUSSION QUESTIONS

1. What do you think of Pete's advice to Mario about the way Mario should behave on the phone when talking to a possible employer?

2. Why do you think it's important to "sound good" on the phone when talking to a possible employer?

STOP *CHECK ANSWERS ON PAGE 116.*

Mario's friend Pete showed him how to practice making phone calls to employers. He offered to let Mario phone him. Pete would pretend to be an employer. In one practice, Mario said he had seen an ad for a job putting together computers.

"Oh yes," said Pete, "we have three openings at our plant. Have you had experience working on an assembly line?"

"I worked assembling parts for cars once," Mario said.

"Our salaries are based on how much experience a worker has," Pete said. "How long did you work assembling car parts?"

Mario hesitated, because he had only worked six months. "A year," Mario said.

Pete told Mario later that he could tell he was lying. "You should have known he would ask you how long you had worked on an assembly line. You should have decided what you would say ahead of time."

"It sounds like I need to think about what questions they might ask," said Mario. "I have been thinking only about what I am going to say myself."

1. Which of the following is the best restatement of the first three sentences?

   a. Pete let Mario use him to practice phoning employers about work.

   b. Mario and Pete took turns pretending to be an employer Mario was phoning for work.

   c. Mario learned how to phone employers by phoning Pete.

GO ON TO THE NEXT PAGE.

2. Which is the best restatement of Mario's last two statements in the selection?

    a. Mario decides to stop thinking about himself and to think more about what others think of him.

    b. Mario feels he should tell employers what he really thinks and less of what might impress them.

    c. Mario realizes he has to think of questions he might be asked instead of things he wants to say.

3. How would you restate Mario's practice interview with Pete? That is, this dialogue:

PETE: (as the employer): Oh yes, we have three openings at our plant. Have you had experience working on an assembly line?

MARIO: I worked assembling parts for cars once.

PETE: Our salaries are based on how much experience a worker has. How long did you work assembling car parts?

MARIO: (He hesitates, because he had only worked six months.): A year.

Restatement:

LIFE SKILLS DISCUSSION QUESTION

What are some good topics for role playing? (Think of specific situations involving parents and children, husbands and wives, employers and employees, grown children and their elderly parents, landlords and tenants, business persons and their customers, government or police people and citizens.)

STOP *CHECK ANSWERS ON PAGE 116.*

LESSON 5

FINDING THE TOPIC OF A PARAGRAPH

One question you probably hear every day is "What is it about?" Someone asks you to tell them what a movie was about, what a magazine article was about, what a meeting or conversation was about. You already have learned how to answer this question by restating. Now you will learn how to find out how to answer the question: "What or whom is the paragraph about?"

The restatements you wrote in the last lesson were about selections that had titles. The titles told you what each selection was about. One selection had the title, "MARIO'S FRIEND PETE GIVES HIM SOME ADVICE." Before you read the selection, you knew the selection was going to be about Pete giving advice to Mario.

Most paragraphs, however, do not have titles. You have to figure out what they are about. What a paragraph is about is called its *topic*. The topic of a paragraph answers the question: What or whom is the paragraph about? The *who* or *what* of the paragraph is the subject of the paragraph.

How do you find the topic of a paragraph?

1. It is a good idea to start by reading carefully the first sentence of the paragraph because the topic is often in the first sentence.

2. Then you can look through the rest of the paragraph to see if a key word or words in the first sentence is repeated. *These repeated words or details are usually clues to what the topic is.*

3. The details in the paragraph should all be related to the topic. In other words, what is being said in the paragraph is about the topic.

Look at the paragraph entitled "HOW MOLLY SAVES MONEY" on page 40. If you read the first sentence carefully, you see that it is about Molly saving money. If you read the rest of the paragraph, you see that every sentence is about Molly and about saving money. The first sentence says: "*Molly* has decided not to get a job for now but to *save money* instead." The second sentence says: "The best way to *save money* is to shop carefully." The third sentence says: "*She* checks prices to make sure she is

GO ON TO THE NEXT PAGE.

getting the *best buy*." ("She is getting the best buy" is another way of saying "she saves money by getting the most for her money.") The next four sentences tell us how Molly uses coupons in supermarkets and "In this way, *she saves a lot of money*." The last three sentences tell us how Molly watches for ads "about sales" and "compares the prices" at different stores and "buys the cheapest items" "so that *she* can *save money* in this way."

You can usually find the topic by reading the first sentence carefully and then by spotting the details that relate to *what* or *whom* the paragraph is about—Molly saving money. The repeated words in the paragraph on page 40 are further clues that the topic of the paragraph is "Molly saving money." All the sentences in the paragraph tell us something about this topic.

Main Points About Finding the Topic of a Paragraph

1. Read the first sentence carefully. Look for *what* or *whom* the paragraph is about.

2. Look for repeated words or repeated details.

3. These repeated details should all be related to the topic.

4. Use only a word or a few words (a phrase), when you state the topic. The statement of a topic is not a sentence.

5. Do not include details in topic statements. The topic "Molly saving money" does not tell us any of the different ways Molly saves money.

Look at this paragraph.

Renting a car is not complicated or difficult. All you need is a drivers license and the money to pay for the car. The car rental agent may check your license to see if you have any serious driving violations and if all the information on it is correct. If you use a credit card, the car rental agent also will check to see if your credit rating is still good.

GO ON TO THE NEXT PAGE.

You also have to sign a paper taking responsibility for any damage to the car you rent. Then you can drive the car for the period of time permitted by the rental.

What is the topic of this paragraph, that is, *what* or *whom* is it about? Read the first sentence. The subject of the sentence, its key phrase, is "renting a car." Next, look for repeated words and details throughout the paragraph. Every sentence (except the second one) contains words that refer to car rentals—"car rental," "car rental agent," "the car you rent," and "drive the car for the period of time permitted by the rental." So the topic must be *renting a car* or *car rentals*.

Look at this other paragraph. First see if you can find the topic of it, that is, *what* or *whom* the paragraph is about.

Bad teenage babysitters create many problems for parents today. Many of these teenagers want more money than the parents can pay for babysitting. These teenagers also want to bring their friends over while they are supposed to be paying attention to the children. Often these babysitters do not stay as long as the parents need them to stay. The worst teenage babysitters put the children at risk by taking them to dangerous places or playing dangerous games with them.

What is the topic? Read the first sentence: "Bad teenage babysitters create many problems for parents today." The most important words are "Bad teenage babysitters," "problems," and "parents." Next, look for repeated words and details throughout the paragraph. Every sentence is about the "bad teenage babysitters" mentioned in the first sentence: "These teenagers," "these babysitters," "The worst teenage babysitters." So the topic must be *bad teenage babysitters*.

Now try writing statements of topics for the following two paragraphs.

GO ON TO THE NEXT PAGE.

Topic Practice 1

What is the topic of the second paragraph in the selection "HOW MARIO GETS MONEY WHILE OUT OF WORK" (on page 29, Unit 1, Lesson 3, Practice 3)?

Topic:

Topic Practice 2

What is the topic of the paragraph with the title "WHAT FOOD MOLLY BUYS FOR HER FAMILY" (on page 42, Unit 2, Lesson 4, Practice 3)?

Topic:

Notice that the statements of topics about car rentals and bad teenage babysitters do not include details. They do not tell what the steps of renting a car are or what bad teenage babysitters do.

Statements of the topic give only the simplest, most basic answer to the question: What or whom is this paragraph about. In other words, the topic of the paragraph is the subject of the paragraph.

Read the following paragraphs and find the topic of each one.

STOP CHECK ANSWERS ON PAGE 116.

Practice 1

Mario hunted for jobs in many different places. He looked at Help Wanted ads in the newspapers. He read neighborhood newspapers as well as city papers. He also looked at ads that were shown in windows of businesses. For example, one store had a sign on the door that said, "Computer repair person wanted." He also looked at the job listings on the bulletin boards in large supermarkets, in clubs, and in community centers. He even looked at Help Wanted ads for part-time work that were on mailboxes, telephone poles, and on the walls of buildings.

Topic:

LIFE SKILLS DISCUSSION QUESTIONS

1. What are other ways that Mario can look for a job?

2. How good do you think Mario's chances are for finding a job? Explain.

STOP   *CHECK ANSWERS ON PAGE 116.*

Practice 2

When Mario found an ad for a job that he thought he could do, he responded to the ad by sending information to the employer about his job experience. If the ad gave a phone number, he responded by calling the company. If the ad gave an address, his response was to write a letter. Either way, he gave them information about his different jobs. He gave some details about what he did in each job. He explained that he had lost his last job because his employer was cutting costs. What he emphasized the most in his response to the ad was why he thought his job experience prepared him for the job the company was offering. Finally, he gave them information about the salaries he had, and he told them how much he would like to be paid.

Topic:

LIFE SKILLS DISCUSSION QUESTIONS

1. What do you think of the information Mario gave when he responded to ads for a job?

2. What kind of information would you give when you answer an ad for a job?

STOP *CHECK ANSWERS ON PAGE 117.*

Practice 3

When Mario finally got an interview for a job, he prepared for it right away. One day at 11:00 A.M., he received a phone call from the Dearborn Company. When he hung up, he told his wife, Molly, that the Dearborn Company wanted him to come in for an interview the next day. He said that he had to start preparing for it right away, so he was going to the library to find information about the Dearborn Company. That afternoon, he went over his notes about the company. After dinner, Molly read them over and then pretended to be the interviewer. Mario practiced answering her questions. When he went to bed, he felt ready for the interview.

Topic:

LIFE SKILLS DISCUSSION QUESTIONS

1. What do you think of Mario's preparation for his job interview?

2. Is there anything else—beyond what Mario does—that you would do to prepare for a job interview? Explain.

STOP *CHECK ANSWERS ON PAGE 117.*

Practice 4

The next day at the interview, Mario explained how his experience made him right for the job. He told the interviewer, Ms. Baum, why he was interested in the Dearborn Company. He said that it was a young and growing company and had made a big profit last year. He continued by saying that it should have many opportunities for young people like himself. He did not ask about health benefits. He already knew about them from an information sheet he had read while he was waiting. He did not ask about the salary because he already had told them what he would accept in his letter. He only asked questions about the job. Ms. Baum seemed impressed. At the end of the interview, she offered him the position.

Topic:

LIFE SKILLS DISCUSSION QUESTIONS

1. How important are health benefits to a person looking for a job? Explain.

2. Why do you think Ms. Baum was impressed with Mario?

STOP *CHECK ANSWERS ON PAGE 117.*

Practice 5

> Mario came back to the Dearborn Company the next day to learn about the company's training program. He met with Ms. Carson who told Mario that they considered training very important there. She said that every level is important and that the company takes time to train all their people. She also said that she feels that is why their people do not leave. She claimed that the cost was well worth it in the long run. She told Mario that his training would take two weeks and that he would have a special "training partner" to help him.

Topic:

LIFE SKILLS DISCUSSION QUESTIONS

1. Do you feel it is important to have a training period to learn about your job? Explain.

2. How do you feel about a company that has a long training period?

3. Do you feel more secure if the company spends time and money to train you? Explain.

STOP *CHECK ANSWERS ON PAGE 117.*

LESSON 6

REVIEW—RESTATING AND FINDING THE TOPIC OF A PARAGRAPH

So far, you have learned ways to get the most from your reading and to put stated ideas together. Let's review them. Then you can practice them.

I. Restating, Part 1—Stating the Meaning of One or Two Sentences in Different Words

You learned to tell when a restatement was correct or incorrect. Look at these sentences and see if you can pick the correct restatement of them.

Statement: He gave them information about his different jobs ... He explained that he had lost his last job because his employer was cutting costs.

Restatement 1: He told them how the job he lost was like the one they were offering.

Restatement 2: He told them his job history and how he lost his last job.

Restatement 3: He told them how he lost his various jobs because of costcutting.

Which restatement is correct? The correct one will be (a) accurate and (b) complete.

Is Restatement 1 accurate and complete? No, the original statement does not say that the man thought the job he lost was like the one they are offering. Therefore, Restatement 1 is not accurate.

Restatement 3 is also inaccurate. The second sentence of the passage says that he lost his last job because of costcutting, but the first sentence does not say that he lost all his different jobs due to costcutting.

Only Restatement 2 is accurate and complete. "He told them his job history" restates "He gave them information about his different jobs," and "how he lost his last job" restates "He explained that he had lost his last job because his employer was cutting costs."

GO ON TO THE NEXT PAGE.

Write a restatement of these two sentences.

Two-Sentence Restatement Practice

Statement: When Mario met the supervisor, Mr. Tanaka, he told Mario the training period was two weeks. An experienced worker in the same job as Mario's would work next to him during that time.

Restatement:

Read this selection and answer the restatement questions about it.

Restating Practice Passage 1

Mario's first day on the job with Clyde, his training partner, turned out better than he thought it would be. For the first few hours, he was nervous. The experienced worker who was next to him did not pay any attention to him. Luckily, Mario had no trouble running his machine. But he also did not have any questions to ask his training partner—the experienced worker. He was afraid that the man would think he was unfriendly. As he worked, he tried to think of something to say to his partner. Then he noticed that a robot was working further down the assembly line. He leaned over to the worker, pointed to the robot, and asked, "Did he have a training partner, too, when he started?"

The worker looked at him as if he were crazy. He told Mario to keep his mind on the job. Mario was worried for a while, but a few moments later the man laughed and smiled at him. When they ate lunch together, his training partner said it would be good to work with someone with a sense of humor.

"I guess my job is safe," said Mario, "because robots don't have a sense of humor, do they?"

"No one's job is safe," said the worker. He became suddenly serious.

GO ON TO THE NEXT PAGE.

1. Which of the following is the best restatement of these two sentences? ("But he [Mario] also did not have any questions to ask his training partner—the experienced worker. He was afraid that the man would think he was unfriendly.")

   a. Mario is afraid his training partner will ask him questions because he has more experience than Mario does.

   b. Mario is afraid to be unfriendly because he needs to have answers to his questions about his new job.

   c. Mario is afraid his training partner will think he dislikes him because he can't think of anything to say to him.

2. Which of the following is the best restatement of Mario's first joke? ("Then he [Mario] noticed that a robot was working further down the assembly line. He leaned over to the worker, pointed to the robot, and asked, 'Did he have a training partner, too, when he started?'")

   a. Mario thinks that the robot is friendlier than his training partner.

   b. Mario wonders if the robot had a training partner, too.

   c. Mario suggests that the robot is a better worker than he, Mario, is.

3. Which of the following is the best restatement of the training partner's reaction to Mario's first joke? ("He [the training partner] told Mario to keep his mind on the job. Mario was worried for a while, but a few moments later the man laughed and smiled at him.") (HINT: Be careful to give a complete restatement.)

   a. The training partner thinks Mario should look for another job.

   b. The training partner is not pleased by Mario's joke but later thinks Mario is funny.

   c. The training partner laughs and smiles but then gets angry at Mario.

GO ON TO THE NEXT PAGE.

4. Which of the following is the best restatement of Mario's second joke? ("When they ate lunch together, his training partner said it was good to work with someone with a sense of humor. 'I guess my job is safe,' said Mario, 'because robots don't have a sense of humor, do they?'")

   a. Mario says robots might take his job because they don't waste time making jokes.

   b. Mario says robots won't take his job because they lack the ability to make jokes.

   c. Mario says he would rather make jokes and be a poor worker than be a humorless robot.

5. How does the training partner react to Mario's second joke? ("'No one's job is safe,' said the worker. He became suddenly serious.")

   a. He thinks it is as funny as Mario's first joke but then he gets angry.

   b. He doesn't think it is funny because it makes him think of losing his job.

   c. It makes him sad because he thinks Mario is going to lose his job.

STOP   *CHECK ANSWERS ON PAGE 117.*

II. Restating, Part 2—Putting Together the Meaning of Three or More Sentences into a Single Statement

Now you will do some larger restatements. You will put the meaning of three or more sentences into one simpler statement. Look at this group of sentences and restate their meaning:

Restating Practice Passage 2

> Mario was very excited. He couldn't believe his good luck. He found a job in a good company that paid well and had excellent opportunities for advancement. The company treated its employees well and had a good training program.

Restatement:

Possible restatement: Mario felt excited and lucky to find a job.

Is this a good restatement? No. It leaves out the most important point: that Mario found a good job. Let's revise the restatement to include this important information.

Restatement: Mario was excited and felt lucky because he found a good job.

You could make the restatement more detailed by mentioning that the job had excellent opportunities and a training program.

However, you do not have to include this much detail. You can write simpler restatements of a passage. You only have to include the most important information: that Mario found a good job.

GO ON TO THE NEXT PAGE.

Write a restatement of the following passage.

> "You know Mario," Molly said several weeks later, "we're lucky that you're collecting unemployment compensation while you're looking for a job."
>
> "I know," replied Mario, "I was thinking the same thing just the other day. At least we have some money coming in every week. That way we don't have to use up all our savings."

Restatement:

III. Finding the Topic of a Paragraph— Finding an Answer to the Question "What or Whom Is This Paragraph About?"

The topic of the paragraph is the subject of the paragraph. The topic of a paragraph is what or whom the paragraph is about: all the details in the paragraph are about the topic. Finding the topic requires you to look at all the details and say what they are about. You do not restate them. You do not sum them up. You give a *name* to "what or whom the details are about."

Remember: in looking for the topic, read the first sentence carefully because the topic is often in the first sentence. See if all the details of the paragraph are related to the topic. All the details of the paragraph should be related to the topic.

STOP *CHECK ANSWER ON PAGE 117.*

Topic Practice 1

What is the topic of the first paragraph of Restating Practice Passage 1 on page 60?

Topic:

Topic Practice 2

What is the topic of the first paragraph of the selection on page 92 (Unit 3, Lesson 8, Practice 2)?

Topic:

In the following passages, you can practice writing restatements and topic statements.

STOP *CHECK ANSWERS ON PAGE 117.*

Practice 1

The second day on the job, Mario had a problem and did not know how to get help. On the assembly line, he was supposed to put a part onto the computer they were making. When one of the computers came down the line, he could not make his part fit onto it. At first, he thought he was not doing his job correctly. Then he thought something was wrong with the computer. Finally, he saw that the part was not made properly. The next thing Mario knew, the computer was moving past him down the line. He knew that he should ask his training partner what to do. Clyde, however, had seen something wrong with his own part. He was working hard to solve his own problem. To fix a serious problem, you were supposed to stop the assembly line. But Mario knew it would be bad to stop the movement of the assembly line. Mario was afraid to tell Clyde about his problem. All of Clyde's attention seemed to be on his own problem. Mario did not know what to do.

1. What was the cause of the problem that Mario had on his job (see sentences 1 through 6)?

Restatement:

2. Why didn't Mario ask Clyde for help? ("He knew he should ask his training partner what to do. Clyde, however, had seen something wrong with his own part. He was working hard to solve his own problem.")

Restatement:

GO ON TO THE NEXT PAGE.

3. Give a restatement of how Mario decided what his problem was (see sentences 3 through 6).

Restatement:

4. Restate why Mario did not know what to do (see last five sentences).

Restatement:

5. What is the topic of this paragraph?

Topic:

LIFE SKILLS DISCUSSION QUESTION

If you were Mario, what would you have done? Explain.

STOP   *CHECK ANSWERS ON PAGES 117 AND 118.*

Mario decided not to ask his training partner for help, which was a mistake. Instead, he decided to ask a supervisor what to do. He walked over to a supervisor and told him that there was something wrong with the part that he was supposed to put on the machine. His supervisor told Mario not to ask him about it but to ask his training partner. His training partner was there to help him. That's why he was there.

Mario went back and told Clyde his problem. Clyde said he should have asked him for help right away.

"I was afraid to stop the assembly line," said Mario. "Besides, you were busy with your own problem."

"There's nothing wrong with stopping the assembly line if you have to," Clyde said. "Your job is not to work fast but to make the computer right. Making a product right is called 'quality control.' Always ask me for help when you need it."

Clyde then stopped the assembly line and found a good part for Mario to use.

1. What does the supervisor say to Mario? See sentences 4 through 6.

Restatement:

2. What reasons does Mario give Clyde for going to the supervisor? ("'I was afraid to stop the assembly line,' said Mario. 'Besides, you were busy with your own problem.'")

Restatement:

GO ON TO THE NEXT PAGE.

3. What does Clyde tell Mario about solving problems on the job? ("'There's nothing wrong with stopping the assembly line if you have to,' Clyde said. 'Your job is not to work fast but to make the computer right. Making a product right is called 'quality control.' Always ask me for help when you need it.'")

Restatement:

4. What is the topic of the first paragraph of this selection?

Topic:

LIFE SKILLS DISCUSSION QUESTION

What are some problems that people who work on assembly lines might have?

STOP *CHECK ANSWERS ON PAGE 118.*

Practice 3

> One day at work, Mario had a coat problem. When he arrived, a supervisor told him to put on a work coat. He showed Mario the dressing room where the coats were. There was no one else in the dressing room. Mario had come to work early because he had not wanted to be late. He put on a coat. In a pocket of the coat he found a box of candy and a small bottle of mineral water. Later, a worker came up to him and told him that he was wearing his coat. Mario told the worker he would give him the candy and the bottle of water. He said, however, that he was too busy to change his coat. The worker started to argue with Mario. Mario began to worry because he saw that a supervisor was watching them. "All right," Mario said, and changed coats with the worker.
>
> "That guy is a troublemaker," his training partner said to Mario. "However, you were right not to waste time fighting with him."

1. Where does Mario find candy and a bottle of water? ("There was no one else in the dressing room. Mario had come to work early because he had not wanted to be late. He put on a coat. In a pocket of the coat he found a box of candy and a small bottle of mineral water.")

Restatement:

2. Restate the problem Mario had with the worker. ("Later, a worker came up to him [Mario] and told him that he was wearing his coat. Mario told the worker he would give him the candy and the bottle of water. He said, however, that he was too busy to change his coat. The worker began to argue with Mario. Mario began to worry because he saw that the supervisor was watching them.")

Restatement:

GO ON TO THE NEXT PAGE.

3. Why did his training partner think Mario was right to change coats with the worker? ("'That guy is a troublemaker,' his training partner said to Mario. 'However, you were right not to waste time fighting with him.'")

Restatement:

4. What is the topic of the first paragraph of this selection?

Topic:

LIFE SKILLS DISCUSSION QUESTIONS

1. Would you have behaved in the same way as Mario? Explain.

2. Do you agree with Clyde that it's best not to waste time with a troublemaker? Explain.

STOP *CHECK ANSWERS ON PAGE 118.*

Practice 4

Mario suggested a change in the way his job was done. He was having trouble putting his part onto the computers that came down the assembly line. He had to put his part under a metal plate and behind some wires on each computer. It was hard for Mario to get under the plate and behind the wires. The worker standing to the right of Mario put the wires onto the computers. All the computers came to this worker before they came to Mario. The metal plate was put onto the computers at the beginning of the assembly line. Mario thought it would be better if the plate and the wires were put onto the computers after—instead of before—he put his part onto them. He told his training partner his idea. Clyde told Mario that his idea would change the whole assembly line, but he suggested that Mario tell the supervisor, anyway, if he wanted to. Mario told the supervisor his idea.

"We have a quality circle every Friday," said the supervisor. "That's where we discuss ideas on how to do things better. Talk about your idea there."

1. What problem does Mario have in putting his part on the computers? ("He [Mario] had to put his part under a metal plate and behind some wires on each computer. It was hard for Mario to get under the plate and behind the wires.")

Restatement:

2. What is the change Mario suggests to solve his problem? ("The worker standing to the right of Mario put the wires onto the computers. All the computers came to this worker before they came to Mario. The metal plate was put onto the computers at the beginning of the assembly line. Mario thought it would be better if the plate and the wires were put onto the computers after—instead of before—he put his part onto them.")

GO ON TO THE NEXT PAGE.

Restatement:

3. What does the supervisor say to Mario about his idea? ("We have a quality circle every Friday," said the supervisor. "That's where we discuss ideas on how to do things better. Talk about your idea there.")

Restatement:

4. What is the topic of the first paragraph of this selection?

Topic:

LIFE SKILLS DISCUSSION QUESTIONS

1. What are some ways that can help you get ahead in a company?

2. What do you think about the supervisor's suggestion that Mario share his idea at the quality circle that meets every Friday? Explain.

STOP   *CHECK ANSWERS ON PAGE 118.*

Practice 5

Mario had a good experience at the quality circle on Friday. All kinds of workers were there—supervisors, experienced workers, and new workers like himself. There were office workers as well as assembly line workers. A boss from the top of the company was also there. He explained to Mario and the other new workers what a quality circle was: it was a weekly meeting where workers tried to solve problems together. The purpose of the quality circle was to find the best way to do the work. Talking together about the best way to do the work would make all the workers feel valuable. That feeling would make them work better. They would make the products better. That would make more money for the company. The more money the company made, the better paid the workers would be. When Mario described his idea, the group discussed it. The boss said that it might be too big a change. He, however, said that they would consider it. He also said that was the purpose of the quality circles. He told Mario that it was good that he already was thinking of better ways

1. In your own words describe what a quality circle is (see sentences 5 through 10 or 11).

Restatement:

2. Who came to the quality circle (see sentences 2 through 4)?

Restatement:

GO ON TO THE NEXT PAGE.

3. What does the boss say are the good effects of a quality circle? ("Talking together about the best way to do the work would make all the workers feel valuable. That feeling would make them work better. They would make products better. That would make more money for the company. The more money the company made, the better paid the workers would be.")

Restatement:

4. What is the topic of this paragraph?

Topic:

LIFE SKILLS DISCUSSION QUESTIONS

1. What do you think of the quality circle at Mario's company?

2. Would you like one at your company? Explain.

STOP *CHECK ANSWERS ON PAGE 118.*

Practice 6

After two months on the job, Mario decided to ask for a raise in pay. He believed that he had three good reasons for getting paid more. First, his idea for changing the assembly line was accepted. Second, he got along well with the other workers. Third, in the quality circle he always was very active. Clyde, his training partner, said to him: "Some day you'll probably be a supervisor."

"I don't want to try for more than I can do," said Mario.

"Don't worry," said Clyde, "they won't make you a supervisor until you are ready."

Then Mario asked Clyde if he thought it was too soon for him to ask for a raise.

"Usually, it would be too soon," said Clyde. "However, your idea for the change in the assembly line was accepted. That was a big thing for you. You should go ahead and ask for more money."

When Mario spoke to the supervisor about a raise, the supervisor said: "I was going to ask the boss to give you one, anyway."

Molly was very proud of Mario when he told her he was getting a raise. "You have come a long way from the time when you were unemployed and were so depressed," she said. "Now we can start planning for the future."

1. Why did Mario decide to ask for a raise (see sentences 1 through 5)?

Restatement:

2. Restate the conversation between Clyde and Mario about Mario becoming a supervisor. ("Clyde, his training partner, said to him: 'Some day you'll probably be a supervisor.' 'I don't want to try for more than I can do.' 'Don't worry,' said Clyde, 'they won't make you a supervisor until you are ready.'")

Restatement:

GO ON TO THE NEXT PAGE.

3. What did Clyde say to Mario about asking for a raise? ("'Usually, it would be too soon,' said Clyde. 'However, your idea for a change in the assembly line was accepted. That was big thing for you. You should go ahead and ask for more money.'")

Restatement:

4. What did Molly say to Mario about his getting a raise? ("'You have come a long way from the time when you were unemployed and were so depressed,' she [Molly] said. 'Now we can start planning for the future.'")

Restatement:

5. What is the topic of the first paragraph of this selection?

Topic:

LIFE SKILLS DISCUSSION QUESTIONS

1. If you were Mario, would you have asked for a raise after two months on the job? Explain.

2. What does Mario's asking for a raise tell us about him? Explain.

STOP *CHECK ANSWERS ON PAGE 118.*

UNIT THREE

LESSON 7

FINDING THE MAIN IDEA OF A PARAGRAPH: PART 1

In the last lesson, you learned how to find the *topic* of a paragraph. You learned that the topic of a paragraph answered the question, "What or whom is this paragraph about?" You learned that the topic is the subject of the paragraph. If all the sentences in a paragraph are about changing a flat tire, the topic is "changing a flat tire." A topic statement is short. It is not a sentence.

What if a friend asked you:

"What does the writer *say* about changing a flat tire?"

"Well," you might answer, "he says you should pull off the road as far as you can. He says you should put out flares. He also says you should look at oncoming traffic now and then while you work."

"Don't give me all the details," your friend says.

"However, they are what all the sentences are about," you say.

"I know," says your friend, "they are all about changing a flat tire. Changing a flat tire is the topic. You told me that already. However, what's the most important thing he says about changing a flat tire?"

Your friend is asking you for the main idea. Every properly written paragraph must have a main idea and only one main idea. The *main idea* is the topic *plus* the most important thing the writer says about the topic. This main idea covers everything in the paragraph. All the sentences develop the main idea, which is the central thought of the paragraph. Think of the main idea as an umbrella—all the details in the paragraph can fit under it without getting wet.

Read the following paragraph and see if you can figure out what the main idea is.

When you are changing a flat tire, make sure you do it safely. First, park your car away from busy parts of the road, such as intersections. Second, park your car as far onto the shoulder of the road as you can, away from traffic. Third, mark the location of your car, so that other cars will see you. Put on your blinking parking lights. If you have

GO ON TO THE NEXT PAGE.

Practice 2

Marissa is having trouble finding a good day care center for her two children. She needs to find one so that she can get a job and go back to school. She has looked at a number of centers, but she was not happy with any of them. They were usually very crowded and the children did not get enough attention from the people taking care of them. Some of the centers were dirty and did not have enough light in their rooms. Others did not have enough toys or other things, like crayons, for the children to play with.

1. What is the topic of this paragraph?

Topic:

2. What is the main idea of this paragraph?

Main Idea:

LIFE SKILLS DISCUSSION QUESTIONS

1. Discuss the day care problem in our country.

2. What suggestions do you have to make it better?

STOP *CHECK ANSWERS ON PAGE 119.*

Practice 3

> Marissa wants to go back to school to learn writing and math so she can get a better job. In school, she can learn to write clearly and correctly. She needs to be able to write good letters to get job interviews. Writing well will prepare her to write business letters in higher level jobs as well. Another thing she will learn in school is basic math. With math skills, she will be able to handle money if she gets a job as a salesperson or as a cashier. Knowing math, she will be able to make a budget for herself. Then, she will be able to save money and plan for the future.

1. What is the topic of this paragraph?

Topic:

2. What is the main idea of this paragraph?

Main Idea:

LIFE SKILLS DISCUSSION QUESTION

What do you think of Marissa's desire to go back to school? Explain.

STOP *CHECK ANSWERS ON PAGE 119.*

Practice 4

> Marissa attends night classes at a community adult education school. Her first class includes all kinds of programs and students. Some students are learning to read English because English is not their first, or native, language. Others are writing or doing mathematics. Some students are studying subjects like history, geography, or one of the sciences, such as chemistry or biology. These students are preparing for the GED exam. The teacher, Ms. Jacobs, goes from group to group and from student to student. After she helps one group or one person, she goes to another student or group of students. The students are of all ages—from teenagers to people who are fifty or sixty years old.

1. What is the topic of this paragraph?

Topic:

2. What is the main idea of the paragraph?

Main Idea:

LIFE SKILLS DISCUSSION QUESTION

What kinds of programs do you think most help adults who are going back to school?

STOP *CHECK ANSWERS ON PAGE 119.*

Practice 5

Marissa's goal is to receive a college education, so she can get a good job. After she passes the GED, Marissa will go on to college. First, she will go to a community college, and then she plans to go to a four-year college. The program in the community college takes two years. Marissa plans to go to this college full-time. A full-time student takes four or five courses in basic subjects like writing and mathematics and other required courses in science, social studies, and literature. A student also takes "elective" courses—courses that he or she does not have to take but wants to take. Any student who studies seriously and gets passing grades usually receives an associate degree at the end of two years of courses. With this degree, Marissa can apply to enter a four-year college. In this kind of college the student usually takes both required courses and elective courses. With passing grades, Marissa will get a bachelor's degree. A bachelor's degree is necessary for most of the better jobs in the United States.

1. What is the topic of the paragraph?

Topic:

2. What is the main idea of the paragraph?

Main Idea:

LIFE SKILLS DISCUSSION QUESTIONS

1. What do you think of Marissa's goal?

2. What are some of your goals?

STOP CHECK ANSWERS ON PAGE 119.

LESSON 8

FINDING THE MAIN IDEA OF A PARAGRAPH: PART 2

In the last lesson, you learned that a paragraph has one main idea only. You also learned that when you put together the topic and the most important thing that the writer says about the topic you have the main idea. The main idea is the central thought of the paragraph. It answers the question, "What is the writer's most important point about the topic?" You learned that all the sentences in the paragraph develop the main idea. You also learned that the main idea is often found in the first sentence.

After you have put together your topic and the most important point about the topic, you should look to see if your main idea is contained in the first sentence. If it is not, it is a good idea to look at the last sentence. There are times when the main idea is found in the last sentence.

Look at this example paragraph.

Mike told Wendy that he wanted to have a place to study. He felt that in their present apartment he did not have such a place. He told Wendy that he needed an office at home because he wanted to start his own business soon. Wendy agreed that they needed more space. She said that she wanted a bigger kitchen and a place to study. She wanted to have her own hairdressing shop some day, so she needed to take courses in small business management. They both also felt that they needed a separate room for their child, Teresa, now that she was getting older. One thing was clear to Mike and Wendy—they needed more space, so their new apartment would have to be bigger than the one they had.

Let's read the paragraph and find out what the topic of the paragraph is. All the sentences talk about *Mike and Wendy's needing more space*. So the topic is *Mike and Wendy's needing more space*. Now let's read the paragraph again and find out the most important thing the writer is saying about Mike and Wendy's needing more space. The most important point made in the paragraph is: *Mike and Wendy's new apartment would have to be bigger than the one they had because they needed more space*. Now let's see if a sentence contains this main idea.

GO ON TO THE NEXT PAGE.

Look at the first sentence. It does not contain the topic and the most important thing that is said about the topic. It states only one detail: the fact that Mike wants a place to study. Other sentences contain details that are about the space that Wendy wants and the separate room that Teresa needs. Now look at the last sentence. Does it contain the topic? Yes, it does. Does it state the most important point that the paragraph makes about the topic? Yes, it does. In other words, does it contain the central thought of the paragraph? Yes, it does. That means it gives us the main idea of the paragraph, the idea that covers all the details in the paragraph: "One thing was clear to Mike and Wendy—they needed more space, so their new apartment would have to be bigger than the one they had."

Look at the following selections and see if you can find the main idea of each of the various paragraphs. *Hint:* In these paragraphs, the main idea may be contained in either the first sentence or the last sentence in the paragraph.

GO ON TO THE NEXT PAGE.

Practice 1

Mike and Wendy have been married and working since they were in high school. They started going together in the ninth grade and got married in the tenth grade. Mike wanted to be an auto mechanic and Wendy wanted to be a hairdresser. In the last year of high school, both of them were in a work release program. They went to school part-time and the rest of the time they worked. Mike worked in his father's garage and Wendy worked in a beauty shop. Two years after they married, they had a child, Teresa. Until Teresa was three, Wendy could not take a full-time job, so she did babysitting. Then, her grandmother started taking care of their daughter and Wendy got work as a hairdresser. Mike had learned on the job and became a full-time auto mechanic.

What is the main idea of this paragraph?

Main Idea:

LIFE SKILLS DISCUSSION QUESTIONS

1. What are problems that individuals who have dropped out of school usually have?

2. What kinds of problems can you foresee for Mike and Wendy?

STOP   *CHECK ANSWERS ON PAGE 119.*

Practice 2

Mike and Wendy had a fight about where to rent a new apartment. They did not think their neighborhood is safe for their little girl. Wendy wanted to move near the neighborhood where her mother and her grandmother live. She felt that it would make it easier for her grandmother to babysit with Teresa and for her to see her mom more often. However, her husband did not like the idea. He did not want to live so close to Wendy's family. He did not want them to visit all the time. Wendy, however, felt this was very unfair because Mike works with his father and sees him every day. They argued until they went to bed.

The next morning, however, Mike called home from work. "It's okay if we move to your mother's neighborhood," he said. "You should be able to see her more often."

Wendy felt lucky to have such an understanding husband.

What is the main idea of the first paragraph?

Main Idea:

LIFE SKILLS DISCUSSION QUESTION

What do you think of Mike's attitude that he does not want to live so close to family? Explain.

STOP *CHECK ANSWERS ON PAGE 119.*

Practice 3

Mike and Wendy's friends suggested a lot of different ways to look for an apartment. First, they asked people they knew how they found their apartments. One friend said to walk in a neighborhood where they would like to live and look for "For Rent" signs. Another friend said to ask all the people they knew if they had heard of a nice apartment for rent. Another friend suggested that they look at advertisements in the "Real Estate" sections in the newspapers. Other friends said that they should do all those things, but they should look for notices for apartments on community bulletin boards, too. Several friends said they might have to go to a realtor—a landlord or agent for several landlords. These people demand a fee for finding you an apartment.

All their friends, however, said, "Take your time. Find an apartment you really like."

What is the main idea of the first paragraph?

Main Idea:

LIFE SKILLS DISCUSSION QUESTIONS

1. What other ways besides those given can you think of to find an apartment?

2. What kinds of things should you consider when looking for an apartment?

STOP CHECK ANSWERS ON PAGE 119.

Practice 4

> In their search for an apartment, Mike and Wendy went to several real estate agents. One was Mr. Fuller. They told him they needed a two-bedroom apartment. Mr. Fuller asked them if they were both working full-time. They both said they were. Then he described several two-bedroom apartments and asked them if they could afford to pay the rents for them. Wendy said that they could pay the rent on the last one he described. Mr. Fuller then said that he was going to paint that apartment and fix it up and he was going to increase the rent because of these improvements. At this point he looked at Wendy and Mike and asked whether they would be able to pay that increased rent. Mike and Wendy felt that Mr. Fuller was mostly interested in how much rent they would be able to pay.

What is the main idea of the paragraph?

Main Idea:

LIFE SKILLS DISCUSSION QUESTION

When going to real estate agents, what are some of the things that you have to be careful about?

STOP *CHECK ANSWERS ON PAGE 119.*

Practice 5

> Mike and Wendy spent a total of two months looking for an apartment. They went to three different real estate agents. All their apartments were too expensive. They walked through many neighborhoods and visited many apartments. They did not like any of them. Then they found exactly the place they were looking for. A friend of Wendy's mother had it. Her mother's friend, Mrs. Berger, was leaving the city to be near her children and grandchildren in Florida. In fact, Wendy's mother heard about Mrs. Berger's apartment from another friend of hers. Mike and Wendy found the apartment they wanted by one of the best methods—by networking through friends.

What is the main idea of the paragraph?

Main Idea:

LIFE SKILLS DISCUSSION QUESTION

What should you consider when trying to figure out if you can afford an apartment (for example, how much you earn, your expenses, and so on)?

STOP *CHECK ANSWERS ON PAGE 119.*

LESSON 9

FINDING THE MAIN IDEA OF A PARAGRAPH: PART 3

In the last two lessons, you learned the two basic steps for finding the main idea of a paragraph: First, you find the topic; then you find the most important thing said about the topic. The topic plus the most important thing said about it gives you the main idea. The third thing you learned was that the main idea is often stated in the first or the last sentence in the paragraph.

This lesson will teach you one more important thing about finding the main idea: *It is possible for the main idea to be stated anywhere in the paragraph.* It may be in either the first sentence or the last sentence of the paragraph. It may be in the second sentence, in the next-to-last sentence, or in a sentence somewhere in the middle of the paragraph. It may be in any sentence in the paragraph.

When you look for the main idea, therefore, you should still use your two basic steps—look for the topic and the most important thing that is said about it. You also should look at the first and last sentences because they probably will give you a clue about what the topic is. Then you should read the paragraph carefully to find out what the most important point about the topic is. After you have your main idea, check to see if all the sentences develop the main idea. Remember, the main idea is the central thought of the paragraph.

Let's see how this works with the following paragraph.

Day care is a problem for many single working parents. Their preschool children often have to attend day care centers that are overcrowded, unclean, and badly run. Many single working parents have to send their children to poor day care centers because they cannot afford good ones. Such centers are cheap but do not have enough money to pay good people to take care of the children. For this reason, the children are frequently left on their own and are not given much attention. Sometimes the caregivers are not sensitive to children and are not well-trained. These inexpensive but bad centers also may lack supplies for the children, such as books, toys, and games.

GO ON TO THE NEXT PAGE.

First, read the paragraph to find out what or whom it is about—the topic. The topic is in the first sentence—the problem of day care for many single working parents. Reread the paragraph carefully. What is the most important thing that is said about this topic? Isn't it that many single working parents have to send their children to poor day care centers because they cannot afford good ones?

Now let's look at each sentence to see if one of them contains our main idea. We also should check to see if our main idea covers all the details in the paragraph. Look at the first and last sentences. Do they contain the main idea? No. The first sentence gives you only the topic—the general problem of day care for single working parents. The last sentence gives you only a detail: It tells you that poor centers lack supplies.

If you look at sentences in the middle of the paragraph, you find other details about the topic. The second sentence says these centers are overcrowded, unclean, and badly run. The fourth, fifth, and sixth sentences describe how the poor centers hire people who do not take good care of the children. None of these statements gives us the central thought that would cover everything in the paragraph.

Is there a sentence that states the main idea covering all these details? Yes, there is. It is the third sentence: "Many single working parents have to send their children to poor day care centers because they cannot afford good ones." The other sentences in the paragraph describe the poor centers these parents are able to afford. This third sentence explains exactly why these parents have a problem with day care. Therefore, it is the most important thing that is said about the topic—the problem of day care for many single working parents. It is the main idea because it covers all the details in the other sentences of the paragraph.

See if you can state the main idea of the following paragraph. Do not look at the commentary following it until you have tried to state the main idea on your own. Read the paragraph carefully.

GO ON TO THE NEXT PAGE.

Recently, many immigrants have come illegally to the United States from Mexico and Central and South America such as El Salvador, Peru, and Honduras. These people are not American citizens and do not have green cards that permits them to work legally in the United States. However, they often are hired, especially as inexpensive day-laborers by employers such as building contractors. They also are frequently hired by people who want housekeepers and nurses for their children but do not want to pay Social Security. Illegal immigrants are becoming an accepted part of American life because they are willing to work for lower pay. These new immigrants may even remind some Americans of their own immigrant parents or their own early years in this country.

Topic:

Main Idea:

Does the first sentence contain the topic of the paragraph? Yes, it does—illegal immigrants in the United States. Does the first or the last sentence give the central thought of the paragraph? No. The first sentence is a detail about where many of the illegal immigrants come from; where they come from is not discussed anywhere else in the paragraph. The last sentence mentions another detail that is not discussed anywhere else—the fact that these immigrant workers remind some Americans of their parents or of themselves when they were new in the United States.

What would you say is the most important thing that is said about these immigrant workers? Wouldn't it be that they cannot work legally but are hired by Americans

GO ON TO THE NEXT PAGE.

anyway because they are willing to work for lower pay? Is there a sentence that covers the main idea? Yes. It is the fifth sentence: "Illegal immigrants are becoming an accepted part of American life because they are willing to work for lower pay." "Lower pay" refers to the details in the third and fourth sentences about "inexpensive day-laborers" and housekeepers and nurses who are not paid Social Security.

The main idea for each of these two practice paragraphs is stated more or less in the middle of each paragraph. However, you would not have known this unless you had already figured out what you felt the main idea should be. Therefore, remember that the best way to find the main idea is to figure out the topic of the paragraph, and then see what the most important point about the topic is. Then, check to see if the main idea is stated somewhere in the paragraph.

Now let's read the following paragraphs and try to state the topic and main idea of each.

GO ON TO THE NEXT PAGE.

Practice 1

Mike and Wendy were very excited about having found the apartment they wanted. Mike and Wendy knew, however, that there were a lot of things they had to do to be able to get the apartment they wanted. They had to set up a meeting with Mrs. Berger's landlord, Stephan Fuentes, as soon as possible. They needed to know what the rent would be. If the landlord raised it a lot, they would not be able to afford to live there. They also had to read the lease to their present apartment again to make sure they could sublet it. If they had the right to sublet—that is, rent out their apartment to someone else—they needed to find a renter who would take it. Once they studied their lease, they would need to talk to their present landlord about moving.

1. What is the topic of this paragraph?

Topic:

2. What is the main idea of this paragraph?

Main Idea:

GO ON TO THE NEXT PAGE.

1. What kinds of things do you think Wendy and Mike should discuss with the landord of the new apartment?

2. What kinds of things should Wendy and Mike discuss with their present landlord?

3. How would you feel about subletting your apartment?

STOP *CHECK ANSWERS ON PAGE 120.*

   1. Write a paragraph about where you live.

   2. State the main idea of the paragraph.

   Check to see if all your sentences develop the main idea of your paragraph. Remember, a paragraph must have one main idea only.

GO ON TO THE NEXT PAGE.

The day before they were supposed to meet their new landlord, Mike and Wendy went to the corner of their apartment they called their "home office." This was the place where they kept their important papers, such as their marriage license and their income tax records. At the desk in their "office" they took out the lease to their new apartment and read it together. Two days before, they had met with a lawyer from a city agency, Joel Carter. He told them to be sure to read their lease carefully before they signed it. He told them that once they signed it, it might be hard to get out of it if they didn't like it later or wanted to move out for some reason. Mike and Wendy could not believe that so many people signed leases without reading them. Joel said that it was true. He also told them that even though the service he was giving them was free—helping them protect their rights as tenants— many people do not take advantage of it. Wendy said that she was surprised because the lease is a contract between the landlord and the tenants. Tenants have to know the law to protect themselves. Joel said that the lease protects the landlord, too. He said that it spells out the rights and the responsibilities of both the landlord and the tenants. Mike and Wendy knew how important it was to know what is in a lease before signing it, so they read their new apartment lease very carefully.

1. What is the topic of the paragraph?

Topic:

2. What is the main idea of the paragraph?

Main Idea:

GO ON TO THE NEXT PAGE.

1. What do you feel a good lease would have in it?

2. Do you think it's a good idea to have someone go over your lease with you before you sign it? Explain.

1. Write a paragraph about the apartment or house of your dreams.

2. State the main idea of your paragraph.

Check to see if all your sentences develop the main idea of your paragraph. Remember, a paragraph must have one main idea only.

GO ON TO THE NEXT PAGE.

The big day arrived. Mike and Wendy were going to meet with their new landlord, Mr. Stephen Fuentes. They were so excited that they caught the wrong bus and took a taxi to make up for the lost time. Mike and Wendy were afraid they were going to be late for their appointment with the landord but everything worked out fine. They actually arrived at the landord's office early. There were so many names on the list of companies in the building where the office was that at first they thought they were in the wrong place. When they told the guard standing by the elevators they were looking for Stephen Fuentes, he said that his office was on the fifth floor, Room 523. Mike, however, felt that it was too early to go up. He didn't want the landlord to think they were overeager—just a couple of kids. He suggested to Wendy that to kill time they should get a soda. The soda machine was at the other end of the building from the elevators. Before they knew it, it was two minutes before their appointment. They rushed to the elevators and luckily got one right away. Mike and Wendy were terribly nervous because the elevator stopped at every floor. When they went in, however, the landlord greeted them warmly. The landlord had a big smile on his face and he told Mike and Wendy that it was nice to meet people who are right on time. Mike and Wendy could hardly keep from laughing out loud.

1. What is the topic of the paragraph?

Topic:

2. What is the main idea of the paragraph?

Main Idea:

GO ON TO THE NEXT PAGE.

1. How do you prepare yourself emotionally for important meetings or interviews?

2. What do you do to make sure you get to places on time? Explain.

3. How do you think Wendy and Mike should dress for the meeting with their landord? Explain.

4. Do you think the behavior of Wendy and Mike is immature or normal? Explain.

STOP *CHECK ANSWERS ON PAGE 120.*

1. Choose a topic.

2. Write a paragraph on the topic.

Topic:

3. State the main idea of your paragraph.

Check to see if all your sentences develop the main idea of your paragraph.

GO ON TO THE NEXT PAGE.

Practice 4

Stephen Fuentes, the landlord, asked Mike and Wendy if they had any questions he could answer. Wendy replied that they did have quite a few. Mike agreed. He started by asking about security deposits. He said that they knew somebody whose landlord refused to return her security deposit. Wendy asked if Mr. Fuentes ever did that. Mr. Fuentes said that he did that once when the tenant damaged the apartment. However, he said that it doesn't happen very often. He said that when a tenant leaves, he usually returns the security deposit, even though legally in their state he has thirty days to give it back. As they questioned him, Mike and Wendy discovered that their new landlord was very fair about the security deposit for their new apartment. Wendy then said that she was curious as to why a friend of theirs had to give a security deposit of one-and-a-half months. She wanted to know if that was against the law. Mike then said that their friend was really upset because it was hard for him to put up that much money plus the first month's rent. Mr. Fuentes replied that it was not illegal. He said that usually the state law says the landlord cannot ask for a security deposit of more than one-and-a-half month's rent. He said, however, that he only asks for a month's rent as a deposit. Mike and Wendy told him they thought that was very fair of him. Mr. Fuentes smiled and said he was happy.

1. What is the topic of the paragraph?

Topic:

2. What is the main idea of the paragraph?

Main Idea:

GO ON TO THE NEXT PAGE.

1. Do you think landlords should require security deposits? Explain.

2. How would you find out whether a landlord was fair? Explain.

1. Choose a topic.

Topic:

2. Write a paragraph on the topic.

3. State the main idea of your paragraph.

Check to see if all your sentences develop the main idea of your paragraph.

GO ON TO THE NEXT PAGE.

As Mike and Wendy got up to leave, Wendy said that she had one more question. It concerned rent increases. She wanted to know if Mr. Fuentes would let them know in advance if there was going to be a rent increase or would he tell them just before the rent is due. Mr. Fuentes said that landlords have to send tenants a notice some time before the rent increase takes effect. He said that it's the law. Mike then remembered a question he had concerning eviction. Mr. Fuentes said that a landlord cannot just evict a tenant—he or she cannot just throw the tenant out. Mr. Fuentes explained that it is really very difficult to evict someone. The landlord must give a written notice to the tenant, not just tell the person to get out. It's also a violation of the housing law to lock someone out of his or her apartment. The landlord has to go to court and get an official warrant that gives a reason for eviction. Mr. Fuentes made it clear to Mike and Wendy that tenants have many basic rights in their relationships with landlords. He said that a landlord cannot even refuse to renew a lease without giving reasons. Wendy then asked what reason would a landlord have for not renewing a lease. Mr. Fuentes replied that the most common reason is failure to pay the rent. Mike said that sounded like a good reason. Wendy, however, quickly said that Mr. Fuentes didn't have to worry because they always pay their bills. At that point, Mike and Wendy signed the lease on their new apartment.

1. What is the topic of the paragraph?

Topic:

2. What is the main idea of the paragraph?

Main Idea:

GO ON TO THE NEXT PAGE.

1. What do you think of the questions Mike and Wendy asked the landlord?

2. Can you think of other questions Mike and Wendy might have asked?

3. What are some ways that you can think of to make sure you get back your security deposit from the landlord?

4. In your area how long before a rent increase does a landlord have to give notice to a tenant?

STOP *CHECK ANSWERS ON PAGE 120.*

1. Choose a topic.

Topic:

2. Write a paragraph on the topic.

3. State the main idea of your paragraph.

Check to see if all your sentences develop the main idea of your paragraph.

ANSWERS

UNIT I
LESSON 1: ANSWERING THE BASIC QUESTIONS
ABOUT SOMETHING YOU READ: WHO? WHAT WHEN? WHERE? WHY?

PRACTICE 1 (P. 5)

1. Mario   2. He got a good job that pays well.   3. last week   4. to a larger apartment outside the city   5. They are saving something out of every paycheck.

PRACTICE 2 (P. 6)

1. Mario's boss   2. He has been laid off.   3. on Monday   4. in his boss's office   5. He was in shock because he didn't expect to be laid off. Just last week his boss had told him that he was a good worker.

PRACTICE 3 (P. 7)

1. Mr. Cortez   2. He wanted to find out why he had been laid off.   3. Business is not good.   4. at the end of the day on Monday   5. in his boss's office

PRACTICE 4 (P. 9)

1. Sam, a co-worker   2. "What's the matter? Are you all right? You look terrible."
3. at the coffee shop   4. a depressed mood   5. He had lost his job.

PRACTICE 5 (P. 11)

1. his wife, Molly   2. walk home   3. after dinner Or: after the children go to sleep Or: right away   4. He walked home.   5. He wanted some time to think. Or: He wanted to figure out how and when to tell the news to his wife.

LESSON 2: READING TO FIND DETAILS

REMEMBERING DETAILS ACCURATELY (P. 15)

1. F   2. T   3. F   4.F

PRACTICE 1 (P. 16)

Networking is calling people you know to help you find a job.
1. T   2.F   3. T   4. F   5. T

PRACTICE 2 (P. 17)

When he networked, Mario phoned all his friends and asked them to help him find a job.
1. T   2. F   3. F   4. T   5. F

PRACTICE 3 (P. 18)

By networking, Mario found out that a company (Or: the Clark Company) was hiring 10 new trainees (Or: had 10 new job openings).
1. F   2. F   3. T   4. T   5. T

PRACTICE 4 (P. 19)

Before the interview, Mario felt very excited.
1. F   2. T   3. F   4. T   5. F

PRACTICE 5 (P. 21)

In his interview, Mario's mistake was that he was not well prepared for the interview.
1. F   2. F   3. T   4. F   5. T

LESSON 3: RESTATING ONE OR TWO SENTENCES

PRACTICE 1 (P. 25)

1. a. Molly thinks it is too early to tell if Mario got the job.   2. c. Molly doesn't think the interview is a fair test of Mario's ability.   3. a. T b. F c. T d. F e. T

PRACTICE 2 (P. 27)

1. c. Mario lost the job because he didn't get ready for the interview.   2. c. Mario should practice being interviewed before an interview.   3. a. F b. T c. F d. F e. F

PRACTICE 3 (P. 29)

1. c. Your level of compensation depends on your pay while working.   2. a. T b. T c. F d. T e. F

PRACTICE 4 (P. 31)

1. b. Mario feels that he is a helpless victim.   2. a. T b. F c. F

PRACTICE 5 (P. 32)

1. a. Molly wants Mario to believe he will have success.   2. c. Molly thinks the children will be afraid and believe Mario is ill if he stays in bed.   3. a. T b. F c. T d. T e. F

UNIT 2
LESSON 4: RESTATING THREE OR MORE SENTENCES

PRACTICE 1 (P. 38)

1. a. They need the money, and she is sure she can get a job.   2. a. Mario cannot look for a job and take care of Eric at the same time.   3. a. F b. T c. T d. T e. T

PRACTICE 2 (P. 40)

1. b. Molly saves money by comparing prices and using coupons to make inexpensive meals.   2. c. With the use of ads to compare prices, Molly finds out about sales at different stores and shops at these.

PRACTICE 3 (P. 42)

1. a. Molly only buys inexpensive meat and fish that she can mix with other inexpensive foods.   2. a. Molly reads labels carefully and buys only healthful foods.

PRACTICE 4 (P. 44)

1. c. Mario thinks employers must want something he does not have to offer.   2. c. Pete wants Mario to show how much he wants to work.   3. Pete tells Mario he must be prepared and sound sure of himself and really interested in the job when he is on the phone talking to a possible employer.

PRACTICE 5 (P. 46)

1. a. Pete let Mario use him to practice phoning employers about work.   2. c. Mario realizes that he has to think of questions employers might ask him instead of things he wants to say to them.   3. During the practice interview, Mario lied about the amount of time he had worked before because his salary in the new job was going to be based on the amount of experience he had.

LESSON 5: FINDING THE TOPIC OF A PARAGRAPH

TOPIC PRACTICE 1: (P.52)

Possible topic: Mario's unemployment insurance compensation

TOPIC PRACTICE 2: (P.52)

Possible topic: Food Molly buys.

PRACTICE 1 (P. 53)

Topic: Mario's job hunt.

PRACTICE 2 (P. 54)

Topic: Mario's response to job ads.

PRACTICE 3 (P. 55)

Topic: Mario's job interview preparation.

PRACTICE 4 (P. 56)

Topic: Mario's job interview.

PRACTICE 5 (P. 57)

Topic: The Dearborn Company's training program.

LESSON 6: REVIEW—RESTATING AND FINDING THE TOPIC OF A PARAGRAPH

I. RESTATING, PART 1

TWO-SENTENCE RESTATEMENT PRACTICE: (P.60)

Possible restatement: Mario's supervisor explained how long the training period would be and who would help him during this time.

RESTATING PRACTICE PASSAGE 1 (P. 60)

1. c. Mario is afraid his training partner will think he dislikes him because he can't think of anything to say to him.   2. b. Mario wonders if the robot had a training partner, too.   3. b. The training partner is not pleased by Mario's joke but later thinks Mario is funny.   4. b. Mario says robots won't take his job because they lack the ability to make jokes.   5. b. He doesn't think it is funny because it makes him think of losing his job.

II. RESTATING, PART 2

RESTATING PRACTICE PASSAGE 3 (P.64)

Possible restatements: Unemployment compensation gives Mario and his wife some money to live on while he looks for a job. Or: Mario and his wife are thankful they have his unemployment compensation while he looks for a job. Or: Mario and Molly can live on his unemployment compensation without using up all their savings while Mario looks for a job. NOTE: The last restatement is probably the best because it is the most complete. It is the only one that mentions that they do not have to use up all their savings. However, the other restatements are also good because they are accurate. They restate the most important information that the unemployment compensation helps Mario and his wife while he is looking for a job.

III. FINDING THE TOPIC OF A PARAGRAPH (P. 64)

Topic Practice 1: Possible topics: Mario's first day on his new job. Or: Mario's first day on the job with his training partner
Topic Practice 2: Possible topic: Mike and Wendy's fight

PRACTICE 1 (P. 66)

1. Possible restatements: Mario couldn't make a part fit onto the computer on the assembly line because the part had something wrong with it. Or: Mario had a problem with a computer on the assembly line because he couldn't make a faulty part fit onto the computer.

2. Possible restatement: Mario didn't ask Clyde for help because Clyde had his own problem with a faulty part.

3. Possible restatement: At first Mario thought he or the computer was to blame, but then he realized that the faulty part was causing the problem.

4. Possible restatement: Mario was confused about what to do because he didn't want to disturb Clyde and he was afraid to stop the assembly line movement, even though you were supposed to if you had a problem.

5. Possible Topics: Mario's problem with the computer on the job. Or: Mario's work problem on the assembly line.

PRACTICE 2 (P. 68)

1. Possible restatement: The supervisor tells Mario not to ask him about problems but to go to his training partner for help with all his problems.

2. Possible restatement: Mario was afraid to disturb Clyde and to stop the assembly line.

3. Possible restatement: Clyde tells Mario that he should always ask him for help and that the most important thing is to do a good job.

4. Topic: Mario's decision about asking for help on the job

PRACTICE 3 (P. 70)

1. Possible restatements: When Mario arrived early for work, he put on a coat that had some items in one of its pockets. Or: When Mario arrived early at work, the coat he put on had a box of candy and a bottle of mineral water in one pocket.

2. Possible restatements: The worker wanted Mario's coat, but Mario was too busy to change coats. Or: The worker said that Mario's coat was his and that he wanted it, even though Mario told him he was too busy to change coats.

3. Possible restatement: His training partner told Mario he was right to avoid arguing with the troublemaker.

4. Topic: Mario's coat problem at work.

PRACTICE 4 (P. 72)

1. Possible restatement: Mario had difficulty inserting his part onto the computer where it was supposed to go.

2. Possible restatement: Mario wants to rearrange the order in which the parts are put onto the computer in the assembly line.

3. Possible restatement: The supervisor suggests that Mario present his improvement ideas to the quality circle that meets every Friday.

4. Topic: Mario's job suggestion.

PRACTICE 5 (P. 74)

1. Possible restatement: The quality circle is a weekly meeting where company people get together to talk about the best way to do the work and how to solve problems together.

2. Possible restatement: Any person in the company can come to a quality circle weekly meeting.

3. Possible restatement: The quality circle helps the workers feel good and be more productive, which increases the income of the company and also benefits the workers. Or: Because the quality circle raises workers' morale and makes them work better, the company makes more money and this then benefits the workers.

4. Topic: Mario's quality circle experience.

PRACTICE 6 (P. 76)

1. Possible restatement: Mario decided to ask for a raise because his idea had been accepted, he got along with everyone, and he was always active in the quality circle.

2. Possible restatement: Clyde believes that Mario will become a supervisor when his bosses think he is ready to become one. Or: Clyde believes Mario will be a supervisor but only when his bosses think he is ready.

3. Possible restatement: Clyde believes that Mario should ask for a raise because the acceptance of his idea for the assembly line was a big deal.

4. Possible restatement: Mario is a changed person and now they can plan for the future.

5. Topic: Mario's decision about asking for a raise.

UNIT 3
LESSON 7: FINDING THE MAIN IDEA
OF A PARAGRAPH: PART 1

PRACTICE 1 (P. 82)

1. Topic: Marissa's unhappy life.

2. Main idea: Marissa has had an unhappy life because of bad luck and a mistake she made.

PRACTICE 2 (P. 83)

1. Topic: Marissa's day care problems.

2. Main idea: Marissa is having trouble finding a good day care for her two children.

PRACTICE 3 (P. 84)

1. Topic: Marissa's desire to go back to school.

2. Main idea: Marissa wants to return to school to learn writing and math so she can get a better job.

PRACTICE 4 (P. 85)

Topic: Marissa's first class.

Main idea: Marissa's first class includes all kinds of programs and students.

Note: Not everything in the first sentence is included in the main idea statement. You usually do not include details in your main idea statement.

PRACTICE 5 (P. 86)

1. Topic: Marissa's goal.

2. Main idea: Marissa's goal is to receive a college education so she can get a good job.

LESSON 8: FINDING THE MAIN IDEA OF
A PARAGRAPH: PART 2

PRACTICE 1 (P. 90)

Main idea: Mike and Wendy have been married and working since they were in high school.

PRACTICE 2 (P. 91)

Main idea: Mike and Wendy had a fight about where to rent a new apartment.

PRACTICE 3 (P. 92)

Main idea: Mike and Wendy's friends suggested a lot of different ways for them to look for an apartment.

PRACTICE 4 (P. 93)

Main idea: Mike and Wendy felt that Mr. Fuller was mostly interested in how much rent they could pay.

PRACTICE 5 (P. 94)

Main idea: Mike and Wendy found the apartment they wanted by networking through friends.

LESSON 9: FINDING THE MAIN IDEA OF A PARAGRAPH: PART 3

PRACTICE 1 (P. 100)

Topic: Mike and Wendy's finding the apartment they wanted.

Main idea: Mike and Wendy knew they had lots of things to do in order to get the apartment they wanted. (See the second sentence.)

PRACTICE 2 (P. 103)

Topic: Mike and Wendy's new apartment lease.

Main idea: Mike and Wendy knew how important it was to know what is in a lease before signing it, so they read their new apartment lease very carefully. (See the last sentence.)

PRACTICE 3 (P. 106)

Topic: Mike and Wendy's appointment with the landlord.

Main idea: Mike and Wendy were afraid they were going to be late for their appointment with the landlord but everything turned out fine. (See the fourth sentence.)

PRACTICE 4 (P. 109)

Topic: Mike and Wendy's questions about security deposits.

Main idea: As they questioned him, Mike and Wendy discovered that their new landlord was very fair about the security deposit for their new apartment. (See the middle of the paragraph.)

PRACTICE 5 (P. 112)

Topic: Mike and Wendy's questions about tenants' rights.

Main idea: Mr. Fuentes made it clear to Mike and Wendy that tenants have many basic rights in their relationships with landlords. (See the seventh sentence from the end of the paragraph.)